WHO PUT A
LIZARD
IN MY LASAGNA?

CHANGE YOUR ATTITUDE, CHANGE YOUR LIFE

SAM GLENN

simple ▶ truths®
LEAD TO CHANGE

Editing by: Alice Patenaude

Photo Credits
Cover: front, murphy81/Shutterstock, abeadev/Shutterstock
Internals: page 1, murphy81/Shutterstock, abeadev/Shutterstock; page 12, Z-art/Shutterstock

Published by Simple Truths, an imprint of Sourcebooks, Inc.
P.O. Box 4410, Naperville, Illinois 60567-4410
(630) 961-3900
Fax: (630) 961-2168
www.sourcebooks.com

Originally published in 2008 in the United States by SamGlenn.com.

Printed and bound in China.

QL 10 9 8 7 6 5 4 3 2

CONTENTS

IS THERE SOMETHING IN THE WAY OF WHAT YOU WANT?

—— ■ ——

Years ago, I only needed a few things—somewhere to sleep, a car that could go from point A to point B (without the assistance of a tow truck), and enough funds to be able to eat and pay a few bills.

It doesn't seem like much on paper, but as simple as securing those necessities might seem to some, I lacked every one of them, and it seemed like a huge struggle to obtain them. The reason "why" was me—I got in my own way. I had a bad attitude and negative thoughts that defeated me in every way possible. Instead of being responsible, I made the choice to criticize and blame others for my unwanted set of circumstances.

At this time in my life, around 1996, my outlook seemed very limited. I had no fuel for my ambition and had endured a series of failures in business and relationships that left me broke, depressed, and angry. There is a saying that we can get better or bitter in life; I chose bitter.

If there was one lesson I learned the hard way, it was that a bad attitude doesn't make great things happen in your life. It deflates your enthusiasm and feeds your imagination with doubt, fear, and anxiety. I still had dreams and goals, but for the time being they were buried deep in the back of my mind. Since my ambition was on pause, so were any opportunities for achievement.

Because I had no steady income, I could not afford my own place. My options were limited. My mother (who was going through some rough times of her own) was kind enough to let me live with her in her small, one-bedroom apartment. I think she felt bad that I had to sleep on the floor in the living room, but I didn't mind. I sort of got used to it. It was much better than trying to fit my six foot six body into the backseat of my car. We made do with the little we had, and I tried to help out where I could. It wasn't easy at the time, but we made it work—mostly Mom did.

The situation reminded me of a quote by Ann Landers: "It is not what you do for your children, but what you have taught them to do for themselves that will make them successful human beings." Those were a rough few years for everyone in the family, but Mom always found a way to make things work, and that equipped my brothers and me with a can-do, make-do attitude.

During this time, I went to a lot of parties, but not the kind of parties you are probably thinking of. They were pity parties, hosted by me. When you have a negative outlook and feel depressed—like there is no way out of the hole you are in—it can be mentally exhausting. I just wanted to eat, sleep, and watch TV, to distract myself from reality. It took every ounce of energy to get my lazy butt up off the couch.

One day, after grabbing the mail, I noticed a brochure featuring an upcoming motivational seminar with guest speakers like Jim Rohn and Mark Victor Hansen. I stopped dead in my tracks as I did a quick overview of the seminar. What got my attention was Fran Tarkenton, the NFL legend who led the Minnesota Vikings to several Super Bowls. As long as I can remember, I have been a die-hard Vikings fan.

I got goose bumps at the idea of being able to meet Fran Tarkenton, let alone hear him speak. I felt a surge of ambition and excitement, feelings I thought had permanently deserted me. My only obstacles were coming up with the $200 to attend the seminar and how to justify paying that amount when I had a mound of debt to pay off. I was earning about $187 a week after taxes, working nights as a janitor. I wasn't sure how I could pull it off, but I felt motivated to find a way.

Fortunately, I had a close friend who wanted to see me get back on my feet and graciously offered to pay for me to go. I was so grateful for that generous gift and still am to this day. It felt good to have something to look forward to. I could taste hope, and it was good.

As an added bonus for registering early for the seminar, I received a set of Jim Rohn's audio cassettes. There were six recordings equaling about three hours, and I listened to all of them in one sitting. His message was awesome! I was so inspired that I started taking notes. I didn't want to forget the value of the wisdom he was sharing! In fact, I still use the information he shared on those audio cassettes to this day.

At that point, my life needed to be refocused. You might say I needed a boot in the attitude. That's something we all need from time to time. If you don't reboot or recharge your attitude battery, it's like trying to start a car when the battery is dead. It doesn't matter how hard you turn that key; if the battery is dead, you aren't going anywhere. Similarly, if you want to perform at an optimal level, you can't do it with a "dead attitude"—you need to reboot.

"I often hear people say,
'I WISH THIS AND I WISH THAT...'
STOP TALKING ABOUT HOW
ONE DAY YOU WILL WRITE A BOOK,
LEARN TO PAINT, START YOUR OWN
BUSINESS, TAKE A CLASS, TRAVEL,
VISIT AN OLD FRIEND, AND

DO IT!

Toss a rock in the air and where it lands,
let that be your starting point. Talking
about it never gets the job done.

DOING DOES!

You may encounter some bumps, detours, road blocks, and rainy days, but you can make great things happen for yourself if you just try...

A LITTLE MORE.

GO DO WHAT YOU WERE BORN TO DO!
LIVE THE LIFE YOU WERE BORN TO LIVE.
DON'T LOOK BACK IN REGRET.
LOOK BACK AND SAY

"I AM GLAD I DID,"

NOT 'I WISH I HAD.'

THAT IS LIVING!"

—SAM GLENN

A NEW DAY...
A FRESH START

— ▪ —

Finally, it was the day of the seminar. Have you ever been so anxious—in a good way—that you could hardly wait for something to happen? I knew in my gut that this seminar would bring a new, better direction for me. I was tired of being tired all the time due to my negative attitude and outlook. Sometimes we get hung up on the past. That doesn't mean we have to live there mentally; we can learn from it and use our past failures as stepping stones.

I was ready to do that. I no longer wanted to use my past as an excuse for not achieving my goals and dreams. Like anything worth pursuing, you have to start somewhere—anywhere. A new day can mean a fresh start.

Registration for the seminar started at 7:00 a.m. and the event kicked off at 9:00 a.m. I was up at 4:00 a.m., out the door at 4:20 a.m., and waiting at the registration table by 5:30 a.m. I was the first one there. Part of my motivation for getting there early was that I wanted a seat in the front row, and sure enough, I got it! When the seminar started, it was even better than I expected.

"What You Want...Wants You More!"

I met each of the presenters and had my picture taken with all of them. It was awesome! I had no money for lunch that day, but I didn't care. I found a quiet spot and starting writing out new goals to improve my life. I had felt stuck and without answers. I didn't know how I was going to turn things around but I was willing to try again, and that was a good starting point.

In the afternoon session, I listened as Mark Victor Hansen dazzled the audience with his humor, stories, and profound thoughts. He then said something that grabbed my attention: "Whatever you want in life, know this... It wants you more."

Wait. What? Say that again! What a profound statement! I need to write this down fast. It wants me more... Huh? I am not sure I understand that.

WHEN YOU **DOUBT** YOURSELF, YOU DEFEAT YOURSELF.

I kept repeating what Mark said over and over. While driving home in Chicago traffic back to my mom's apartment in Naperville, Illinois, I tried to wrap my mind around that statement. It really stuck with me. *Was it just a fancy way of saying that if you want something in life, then get up, do what needs to be done, and go get it?* Yep, it was!

I felt I had a lot of potential to learn new skills that would help me achieve what I wanted in life. However, in the back of my mind, there was some doubt because I didn't have a lot of resources—I was cash poor, and any extra money I earned went to college loans or overdue credit card bills. I recall thinking, *If I don't have the resources, how am I going to achieve what I want?*

But I was asking the wrong questions, those that only fed my doubts. The lesson I learned is: **when you doubt yourself, you defeat yourself.**

There had to be a way to achieve what I wanted by playing the cards I had—with my knowledge, skills, education, and abilities. So, I began to inventory my talents and craft a plan for implementing my goals. After writing it all down, I realized I *did* have a lot to offer and could start to put something positive in motion.

Over the years, my list of needs, goals, and dreams changed considerably, but along the way, I picked up a few lessons that supported my efforts, helping me to achieve what I want by using the best of who I am.

The lessons I learned are simple and changed my life for the better. It all started as a fun prank by my mom. Here is what happened next...

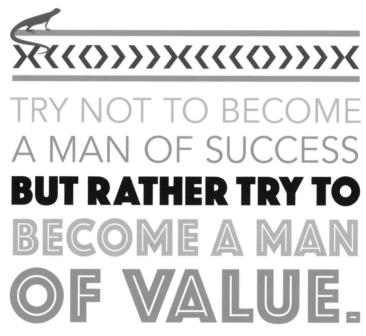

TRY NOT TO BECOME A MAN OF SUCCESS **BUT RATHER TRY TO** BECOME A MAN OF VALUE.

—ALBERT EINSTEIN

A PRANK GONE GOOD!

In 1999, I was finally able to afford my own one-bedroom apartment near downtown Naperville, Illinois. My speaking business was in its early stages but definitely gaining momentum. As a way to become more attractive to potential clients, I did a lot of speaking engagements for free. Sometimes that was difficult, because as my landlord would happily inform me, "Free don't pay the rent."

My business really took off after Billy Graham's grandson heard my speech at a fund raiser and invited me to speak at some of their events. Eventually, I earned enough income to stop working nights as a janitor on the graveyard shift. That was great because working as a janitor wasn't easy. I worked for eight to twelve hours, came home as the sun was rising, and slept for about five hours. As soon as I would wake up, I would start working on my goals.

Back in those days, I was a regular at Dunkin' Donuts. In fact, the smell of coffee still reminds me of those times. I would sit at a table with my coffee, journaling my ideas and game plans on a legal pad. I reminded myself that I have what it takes and that if I kept a positive attitude, worked hard, and did the right things, anything was possible.

I was king of my new one-bedroom castle but a lousy cook. I burned everything. Once, I thought it would be nice to treat myself to a nice steak from the butcher, so I brought it home, put it in the microwave, and cooked it until it shrank into bite-sized beef jerky. My treat could only be used as a doorstop.

I was hungry for food that didn't taste like ashes from a fire. I think mothers can sense when their boys are hungry, but if my mom couldn't, I am sure all the messages I left her did the trick. "Hey, Mom. Do you hear that rumbling? It may sound like a monster, but it's just my stomach letting you know how much it enjoys your food."

My mom and stepdad, Andy, would sometimes pop over, and I could not have been happier. I enjoyed my time with them and we laughed a lot. An added bonus was when they brought grocery bags filled with toilet paper (which you can never have enough of and leftovers, which I call "aged home cooking."). One of my favorite dishes is lasagna, which was like hitting the jackpot. I'd reached the end of the food rainbow!

One particular morning, after receiving a fresh shipment of leftovers, I sat down to enjoy a hefty slice of cold lasagna. Little did I know that my tasty Italian dish contained an added and unrecognizable ingredient. My mom's heartfelt addition created an impact that would eventually become my message to millions, giving birth to a concept that would help me become a successful business owner and enrich the quality of my relationships.

KIND WORDS WILL UNLOCK AN IRON DOOR.

—TURKISH PROVERB

IS THAT A LIZARD IN MY LASAGNA?

It's slightly disturbing to find something unexpected in your food, but this unexpected addition really helped to change my life.

Mom's lasagna was on my brain. I had my fork, a napkin, and a big appetite. My only hope was that Mom didn't put black or green olives in the lasagna. As a boy, I would always ask, "Mom, are there olives in this lasagna?"

Her response: "Nope!"

"Are you sure?"

"Yes, Samuel. There are no olives."

"Okay, if there are, you know I will probably puke at the dinner table, right?"

"Samuel Richard Glenn, you will not!"

"Well, if there are olives in the lasagna, then it could happen!"

"Well, it better not, mister!"

Then, two minutes into eating the lasagna, I would find part of an olive!

"What the...?! Mom, I thought you said there were no olives?"

"Oops, I'm not sure how that got in there. Just pick them out."

"YUCK!"

Mom had assured me that there were no olives in the leftovers she sent, but that didn't stop me from examining things, just to make sure. After I rolled back the tinfoil to dive into the dish, staring up from the top noodle was a **four-inch lizard**!

I don't recall if I screamed or jumped back, but my thought was, *What is that thing?! This is so much worse than olives!* As shocking as it was, it made me laugh and think, *Mom baked a lizard into the lasagna! That crazy lady! Why did she do this?*

I picked it off the pasta to discover it was a plastic toy. It had a long tail and a silly grin. I made a quick call to Mom.

"Mom, did you put a lizard in the lasagna?"

She laughed. "I did!"

"Why did you do that?"

"Because I thought it would be funny! Did you laugh?"

"I did!"

"Then it worked!"

I remember thinking that it really made my day. It felt good to laugh about something silly and not obsess about life's difficulties for once. That was the start of something that would, oddly enough, become known as the "lizard experience"—a new way of looking at life that allowed me to use what I had to achieve a different, and better, result.

I ate the lasagna with my new friend looking on. The lizard quickly became my apartment mascot. I didn't think much of it at first, but then it hit me. Mom was being silly, so why not have some fun and return the favor? Why not create the same unique experience for her?

During my next visit, I snuck into the bathroom and put the lizard in the back corner of the shower, thinking it would create a good scream and laughter later. I returned home, anticipating the response. I wanted to call them and say, "You guys stink. I can smell you from here. Go shower!"

I was anxious to hear what their reaction was. A few hours passed and, sure enough, I got the call.

"Samuel! Did you put that lizard in the shower?"

"I did! Did you laugh?"

"I did!"

"Then it worked!"

The experience was a hit! After that, I thought we were done with the reptilian toy. Mom had a different agenda. She turned into Dr. Frankenstein and gave that lizard a life of its own. She somehow snuck it back into my apartment again for me to find as a surprise— wrapped up in a toilet paper roll!

That time, I didn't say a word to Mom. I just returned the prank again. That four-inch lizard found its way back and forth in different locations in our homes for more than a decade. That lizard has been hidden in more unique places than you can imagine. It created an experience that strengthened our relationship, but also brightened our days. That alone was enough reason to keep doing it; it was fun. However, the experience started revealing life lessons I could benefit from that I share with hundreds of audiences in my speeches. And, I'd like to share them with you.

THOSE WHO BRING **SUNSHINE** INTO **THE LIVES OF OTHERS** CANNOT KEEP IT **FROM THEMSELVES.**

—JAMES M. BARRIE

THE LIZARD CREATES MEMORABLE EXPERIENCES

Smart business is all about creating memorable experiences for your customers so they tell others and come back again and again. Personal relationships blossom when you create the gift of experiences that becomes treasured, such as when Mom and I hid the lizard for each other. To create those experiences, you have to have purpose.

For example, on a cold, rainy afternoon in Duluth, Minnesota, I was running late and was trying to find a cab to take me to the airport. I finally hailed one, jumped in the backseat with my carry-on luggage, and said, "Airport, please."

As we sped away, something moved on the back shelf under the rear window. People often store things there, so I didn't think much of it until I glanced over my shoulder. I saw something that looked like a three-pound rat! I did a double take and leaned away from the creature in total surprise.

"Excuse me," I said to the driver. "Is that a rat in your car?"

He started laughing and, with an accent I couldn't quite place, said, "No! No! Dat's no rat! Dat is a Chew WA WA!"

"Excuse me, a what?"

"Jou knows…a Chew WA WA!"

"Oh, a Chihuahua."

"Yeah! A Chew WA WA."

"Wow, he kinda looks like a big rat. Is he friendly?"

"Dat dog is old, but he got a good life."

Peering into the rearview mirror, he then said words that I didn't quite understand at first.

"Hey! Let hem licka your face, ah!"

"Huh?"

"Let hem licka your face!"

Stalling, I asked, "Um… Why should I let him lick my face?"

"Because it-a make-a you feel soooo good."

"Hmmm…Really?!!"

The ratty-looking dog was already by my face, so I reluctantly leaned in and said, "Hello, fella." The balding dog jumped into my lap, stood on his hind legs, and began licking with what I could only define as passionate enthusiasm. At first, I was resistant, and for good reason—two minutes before, I thought he was a rat!

It was the enthusiasm of the dog that got to me. He was one-of-a-kind, and his attitude was contagious. The cabbie also played a big role. He understood the value of creating memorable experiences using the best of what he had.

By the time we got to the airport, I was practically licking the dog back! Not really, but I like to tell people that. When I got out of the cab, I felt better than when I first got in. The experience had improved my outlook for the day. It was just what I needed.

Let's expand on this lesson just a bit more. There are perhaps a hundred cabbies in the

USE THE BEST OF WHAT YOU HAVE
(a loving and enthusiastic dog)
TO CREATE THE BEST OF WHAT YOU WANT
(more business and loyal customers)

Duluth area. But whenever I go back and need a cab, I don't want just any cab, I want the one that created an experience worth returning to. I want the one with the "lickin' Chihuahua."

As a result of my experience, the cabbie got a generous tip and gained a customer who would return for future business. He used the best of what he had (a loving and enthusiastic dog) to create the best of what he wanted (more business and loyal customers). Whether you are in business for yourself or work for a company, isn't that what you want as well?

This is the basic premise of the lizard experience.

It's about using the best of what you have, wherever you are, and applying it to everything you do with a positive attitude.

I BEGAN LEARNING LONG AGO THAT **THOSE WHO ARE HAPPIEST ARE THOSE** WHO DO THE MOST **FOR OTHERS.**

—BOOKER T. WASHINGTON

USE WHAT YOU HAVE TO THE BEST OF YOUR ABILITY

To determine what you can use in your efforts to achieve what you want, you have to take inventory of your strengths, gifts, talent, education, skills, and abilities. Determine what you have and use it to be your best. But remember to do it with the right attitude. A negative attitude will weaken the performance of your strengths.

So what do you have that you can use right now? Have you ever really thought about it? Are you dependable, honest, consistent, open-minded, respectful, teachable, a team player, energetic, hardworking, or caring? Those are all dynamic strengths.

Here are mine as an example:

1. *I am creative and use that creativity to find solutions to problems.*

2. *I have a good sense of humor that helps me connect with others and deal with stress.*

3. *I am a hard worker.*

Can you list your top three strengths?

Take a moment and think about how you can better use your unique strengths to bring more value to your profession or to your relationships as a friend, parent, or spouse.

Here's an example that will bring the point home. I drove an '82 Buick Regal well past 1982. Believe it or not, I named this car Betty. She was a rusty brown color, drove like a boat, and had a bad cough, but it was a good car for my budget. Some days, Betty showed her age; others, she ran well. I had a bittersweet relationship with Betty. I loved having a car but hated wondering if something else would go wrong. Have you ever been there? It is frustrating.

During the times Betty gave me trouble, I wanted to complain and stop caring for her. It wasn't always easy, but instead of complaining,

I made the decision to do the best I could with what I had. I kept the interior clean by throwing out all the trash. I washed Betty as often as I could and did what was necessary to keep her running. For a beat-up '82 Buick, I made Betty look as good as anyone could.

Eventually, something inside of me said, *Sam, you were a good steward and did the best you could with the resources you had. Now you are financially ready to advance.*

When you do the best you can with what you have and do so consistently, there comes a graduation point. Because I maintained my old car, I felt I deserved a new one. So that's exactly what I got! It is better to deserve something as a result of your effort than to get something out of an attitude of entitlement. I was sorry to see Betty go, but it was time for me to move onward and upward.

THERE IS NO GROWTH IN GETTING something out of SIMPLE ENTITLEMENT.

IT HAS MORE MEANING when you know you EARNED IT.

Some might argue, "Well, if you wanted a new car, you could have gotten one no matter what shape your last car was in." That is true. But when I got the new car, I felt more deserving of it because I made the best of what I had in my previous car. My dedication to taking care of what I had made the experience of getting a new car more rewarding for me.

There is no growth in getting something out of simple entitlement. It has more meaning when you know you earned it. It makes all the difference! When I got my new car, I was so grateful for it that I extended the best treatment I could to it as well. I used the best of what I had to create the best of what I wanted.

I've applied this principle in my approach to work as well.

I've cleaned toilets, washed floors and dishes, delivered newspapers, worked straight commission, served ice cream, done door-to-door sales, cut lawns, loaded trucks, pumped gas, painted, answered phones, ran errands, sold furniture, waited tables, framed pictures, and assembled products. I've worked with negative people and had negative bosses. Did I always like the work? Honestly, I can say no. It was work, and that's all it was. I was there to do the jobs and get the paychecks. That was the deal I had with my employers. However, I learned that if I complained and became negative like everyone around me, then I would give less than my best and never move onward and upward.

So what moved me forward? I changed my perspective from a perception that those jobs were using me to a perspective that I was using them—to learn, grow, and become more valuable in the workforce. I stopped seeing my work as unimportant and started seeing it as a tool to get better. I watched people in leadership roles and saw what worked for them and what didn't.

I sought ways to add value to my position by doing more than what was required and doing it the best I could. In doing so, I eventually "graduated" and moved on.

Was it easy? Not at all. Will it be easy for you? The Magic 8 Ball says, "Don't count on it!" Nothing worth achieving is ever easy or it wouldn't be worth going after, right? Achievement requires that you do your part. It can be a bumpy road, but if you stay on track and use your strengths with a positive attitude, you will advance.

THE STARTING POINT OF ALL

ACHIEVEMENT IS DESIRE.

—NAPOLEON HILL

THE LIZARD CREATES AND NURTURES CONNECTIONS

L ife is empty without quality relationships. The lizard created a deeper connection between my mom and me. When either of us finds the lizard, we know it's an expression of love that nurtures our relationship as mother and son.

Relationships require attention, and that leads to connection. Whatever you give attention to grows; whatever you ignore loses strength. When you value something, you must invest the time to nurture it.

Like repeatedly hiding the lizard, it's a matter of developing joyful rituals. After one of my speeches, a woman told me that instead of a lizard, her family does the same thing with a colorful sock. They each take turns wrapping and randomly giving it to someone in the family for the holidays each year. She said they started doing

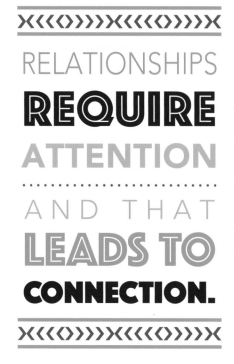

RELATIONSHIPS **REQUIRE** ATTENTION AND THAT LEADS TO **CONNECTION.**

it for birthdays or for no reason at all other than to have a little fun.

At the end of my speeches, I like to give everyone a toy lizard to remind them that we all have something valuable to give. A positive attitude makes great things happen. One woman who had attended my speech emailed to tell me that she took the plastic lizard I had given her and passed it to her six-year-old son. She told him the story about the lizard experience and how hiding it for someone to find is a fun way to express love. The next day when she got to work, she opened up her briefcase and found the lizard on top of her papers!

The key to the lizard experience is sincerely nurturing a deeper connection with someone. It's not about manipulating others to get what you want or wondering, *If I do this, what will I get out of it?* It's about being genuine, authentic, and real—thinking about someone else's needs before your own.

There are several unique ways in which we can nurture our personal or professional relationships. We can give words of encouragement, call someone, do a favor, recognize them in front of peers, treat others to lunch, or send a gift card or special occasion card to let others know we remember them.

One of the best things we can do to deepen our relationships is just listen. Sometimes people don't want anything more than a listening ear so they can vent or just decompress from some aspect of life. There are many things we can do to add meaning to our relationships. Make a list of people who mean the most to you and jot notes beside their names as a reminder of what you can do to brighten their days.

Often when I have a speaking engagement, I have a long drive ahead of me. So I make a list of people I want to call before I head out the door. Even if I don't get them in person, I leave them a classic Sam voice mail, one filled with humor. They will make you smile and want to listen to them over and over again. Stop, think of someone, and take time to nurture your relationships using the best of who you are.

Make Time to Spend Time

I am no relationship expert, but I do know that we can't go through life or succeed alone. Without meaningful relationships, life itself becomes meaningless and what we achieve lessens because we don't have someone to share it with.

One way I like to build positive relationships is by meeting friends for breakfast at our favorite café. My schedule is pretty busy, but when I get a free moment, I like to enjoy a nice cup of coffee, two eggs scrambled, a side of bacon, and the company of good friends.

During our breakfast, we share thoughts, opinions, hardships, encouragement, or whatever is going on in our lives. We laugh and joke, offer advice, or just listen. When we walk out after the meal, we walk out full—and not just from the food.

There is no substitute for time spent building relationships. List how you can _make time to spend time_ with the following people:

* Neighbor

* Boss

* Friend

* Coworker

* Golf buddy

* Playdate mom

* The jogger you wave at every morning

THE WORLD IS
BUT A CANVAS

. . . .

TO OUR IMAGINATION.

.... —HENRY DAVID THOREAU

THE LIZARD AWAKENS CREATIVITY

For well over a decade, surprising my mom by finding new places to hide the lizard has been a challenge. We never hid the lizard in the same place. The lizard experience is about being creative—unlocking your imagination and being open to new possibilities.

We all have the ability to be creative. It may take some time to develop, but the ability is there. You just have to activate it. Think back to when you were a child. As a little boy, when I got my hands on a box of Crayola crayons, I was creative on paper, on the walls, in the bathroom sink, the car, the driveway, and, amazingly enough, all over myself! Being creative is an artful expression of who we are. We can create solutions, turn ideas into reality, and make a way where there seemed to be none.

WHEN YOU CHOOSE TO USE YOUR CREATIVITY, YOU USE THE BEST OF WHO YOU ARE TO ACHIEVE THE BEST OF WHAT YOU WANT.

Sometimes you have to **rethink** what you are doing and make some creative modifications.

For example, Starbucks did something I thought was really creative. It is pretty common to forget your cup of joe on top of the car while you unlock the door. A Starbucks associate attached a fake cup of coffee on the roof of a car and drove around the city. People kindly yelled out, "Hey! Your coffee is on your roof!"

For every person who said something, the Starbucks associate handed out a coupon for free coffee. That is genius. Not only did it create a new way to get customers in the door, but the story also got national media exposure. How cool is that? Starbucks used a little creativity to achieve their goal.

An Act of Creativity Can Make Someone's Day...or a New Customer

When I was setting up my company with a payroll plan, we got many calls from sales reps who wanted to get our business. I got calls, emails, letters, and postcards. However, one company representative did something very creative and out of the ordinary for her sales pitch. She purchased a pie, brought it to our company, and taped a note to the box saying, *I am hungry for your business!* I was so impressed with her creativeness, she got the business, and I ate the pie!

I use creativity in my own business as well. When I officially started my speaking business in 1998, I had zero budget for marketing or business cards. It forced me to think more creatively than other speakers to help me get my foot in the door and obtain new business.

Sam Glenn, The Attitude Guy www.SamGlenn.com

For example, nobody has a business card like mine. Most business cards look the same, but mine pops. It tells people what I do and is funny and memorable. As a result, people hold on to it and share it with others because it's so unique and creative.

Everything begins as a creative idea. When you choose to use your creativity, you use the best of who you are to achieve the best of what you want. It can open doors where there seem to be none.

Creative Solutions

People love good news, but it is common, almost expected, to expect bad news, especially when dealing with corporations. If you want to build business, learn to give people good news.

But what if there is none? Then find ways to make a poor situation better. It takes creativity and effort, but you'll set yourself apart from all your competitors.

For example, I often find myself inconvenienced when I try to check into a hotel and my room isn't ready when I am. One time, though, I dealt with a registration clerk who understood "lizard" creativity.

The clerk could have said, "Your room isn't ready. Can you come back in a few hours?" As you can imagine, I've heard this too many times. But this particular person offered me some better news.

"Mr. Glenn," he said, "I am so sorry your room isn't ready. We would like to treat you to lunch and some of the best-tasting desserts you'll ever have. I don't expect you'll have to wait much longer, but if so, I'll let you know. We'll do our best to make you comfortable until your room is ready."

This wasn't a four-star hotel. It was simply a place that understood how to create an experience worth returning to. The fresh, innovative approach to a common problem caught me entirely off guard—and made a potentially grumpy situation into a pleasant one.

That's how you build business and positive relationships.

Keeping the Customer Happy

Sometimes, inconvenience takes a more serious turn. Once, my flight from Reno to Boston was delayed for hours and then finally canceled.

Since I needed to get to a speaking engagement scheduled for the next day, I was upset and frustrated. Not only had this already wasted a huge amount of my time, but it also threatened my income and professional reputation. The irritation factor was high, and so was my blood pressure!

When I finally reached the counter to start the rebooking process, I really didn't know what to expect. The woman helping me said, "I am really sorry about this. We can get you out first thing in the morning and are upgrading you to first class."

It wasn't an ideal solution, but she repackaged the information into a good-news format. She could have said, "We can't get you out until tomorrow. It's not my fault. I don't control the weather." The lack of an apology would have upset me more, and the negative format would only have confirmed my worst thoughts.

CREATIVE THINKING IS SIMPLY A WAY TO MAKE BAD NEWS, GOOD NEWS.

Instead, she was sincere and spun the bad news to focus on the positive. She let me know that the airline knew the situation was upsetting and possibly damaging to my plans. Then, she guided my attention to the better news: I'd leave on the first morning flight, in time to make my engagement, and I'd be more comfortable flying first-class.

The next time you face a difficult situation, think about how you might offer information in the form of good news. Using creative thinking, it's a simple way to remedy situations that might be out of your control.

Psychologist Erich Fromm says, "Creativity requires the courage to let go of certainties." Although we may feel certain that we'd like to do something nice for someone, we may feel we can't because our resources are too limited. But, if you are creative, you don't need a lot of money.

For example, some of my friends were short on cash and thought that date night might not be a good way to spend their limited resources. But, instead of staying home, they visited a really nice hotel in their hometown and had coffee in the hotel's café. By looking at old places in new ways, they found a fun way to relax. They took the best of what they had—Chicago's nice hotels—to create the best of what they wanted—an inexpensive, fun night together, people-watching. Open your mind and your life to new people, places, and actions. Or, see the same people, places, and things around you in a new way. You'll be surprised what you find.

WE MAKE A
LIVING BY
WHAT WE GET,

·

BUT WE MAKE A
A LIFE BY WHAT
WE GIVE.

–UNKNOWN

THE LIZARD REVEALS PURPOSE

When my mom and I were on our secret missions of hiding the lizard for each other, we did it with purpose, and it felt great. Our mission was to surprise each other and make each other's day.

The great thing about connecting to a purpose is that it creates enthusiasm and meaning. We all want to feel that what we do in life, whether in our jobs or our personal lives, has purpose. Sometimes it takes a while to discover the purpose in our efforts, but if we look with the right attitude, as my mom and I do when hiding the lizard, we see passionate purpose unfold.

There Is Purpose in Knowing What Is Unique about You and Using It in Positive Ways

I learned this lesson from my friend, Larry Winget, bestselling author of several books, including *Shut Up, Stop Whining, and Get a Life.* I attended one of his meetings in Scottsdale, Arizona, to help my speaking business. It was awesome, and I learned a lot. While Larry was eating lunch with his wife, I became that annoying guy who just pulls up a chair without asking. I guess I was just hungry to learn. During lunch, he offered me this advice:

"Sam, discover what is unique about you and exploit it. Market it like crazy. Don't try to be like me or anyone else. Be your uniqueness."

He's right. People try to copy others. There's a perception that if we copy a successful person, we'll feel more valuable and reach the same level of success. But modeling success is about modeling actions. It's not about losing yourself or your own personal brand.

Choose to Be the Best Version of Yourself, Not a Second-Rate Version of Someone Else

When you discover your uniqueness, you need to put it into action. By doing so, you will find more purpose in life and be more effective. You'll take pride in your efforts, so that instead of cutting corners, you'll do the right things. Finding purpose elevates your performance.

I learned this lesson at a job I got at a gas station just after graduating from high school. My manager had just come from another store to turn ours around. You could tell by his attitude that he was a superstar. He made others feel important, and he communicated the value of treating each customer in an exemplary way. I can honestly say he made my experience an enjoyable one. His example rubbed off as I began to take more pride in what I was doing.

> As a leader, these attributes —
> **CONFIDENCE,**
> **PERSEVERANCE,**
> **WORK ETHIC AND**
> **GOOD SENSE —**
> are all things I look for in people.
>
> **I ALSO TRY TO**
> **LEAD BY**
> **EXAMPLE**
> **AND CREATE AN**
> **ENVIRONMENT**
> WHERE GOOD QUESTIONS
> AND GOOD IDEAS
> can come from anyone.
>
> —HEATHER BRESCH

Most people would assume that a job at a gas station is an ordinary one. But my manager created such a positive perspective that everyone who worked there felt connected to our purpose. It was really cool to witness this culture in action.

The only hang-up I had with the job was the uniforms. They were awful red smocks with unidentified and disgusting stains. They didn't look attractive, and when I was wearing mine, I didn't feel important; I felt lowly. So I decided to take the initiative that was inspired by my manager. Instead of putting on the ugly smock, I wore a nice shirt and tie to work. I dressed with purpose and to impress. I wanted to look professional and presentable, even if I was just pumping gas, cleaning bathrooms, and working the register. Dressing up made me feel more confident, and it sent a great signal to those around me. My professional look impressed my manager. He loved it and encouraged it. I had a sense of pride in my job and was more motivated to be my best.

Then, something happened that I never anticipated. Some regional executives stopped in one day. They were so impressed with how I looked and acted, they approached me about becoming a manager one day. I told them I had a great role model; my manager was amazing!

Then, one morning, everything changed. My manager was promoted after only six weeks. He had turned things around quickly, making our store exemplary with its clean, fast, and friendly service. Then, we met the new manager. I knew it was a bad situation the moment he showed up—forty-five minutes late. He wasn't very friendly, and his shirt was wrinkled with odd stains on it. He was not an example of excellence. He was the poster child for what not to do in a quest for success!

The situation got worse when he pulled me aside for a fireside chat. He told me I had to wear the required uniform, the ugly red smock, and that he'd better not catch me without it on or there would be consequences.

You could just hear the purpose, confidence, and positive attitude draining out me. I tried to counter his demand, "But doesn't the nice ironed shirt with no stains and nice tie look better?"

"It's company policy," he said. "Do it."

To say the least, everything changed when I put on the red smock again. My smile went away, my desire to do a good job vanished, and my excellence went into hibernation. Two weeks later, the new manager got fired. He just didn't get it, and he didn't make people feel valued or help them connect to a sense of purpose.

By that point, it was time for me to go on to college, but I did take a valuable lesson from the entire experience. The first manager's commitment to excellence created excitement in everyone around him. I learned that fostering excellence starts a domino effect and creates a better work environment for others.

That's using the best of what you have to achieve the best of what you want!

EXCELLENCE
IS NOT A SKILL.
IT IS AN
ATTITUDE.

—RALPH MARSTON

THE LIZARD IS HUMOROUS AND FUN

When we feel good, we are kinder and more attentive to the positive things in our lives

Who doesn't love to laugh and have some fun once in a while? It's good for you, and it's good for others. Almost every time I find the lizard in an unexpected place, it makes me laugh. It is so unexpected but fun at the same time. One time, I pulled out my wallet to show my ID to the person checking me in for a flight, and wouldn't you know it, the lizard made an appearance. There it was, on top of my driver's license. The airline representative looked at the lizard, then at me, and we both started laughing. As soon as she started laughing, her coworkers looked to see what she was laughing at. You could just see it in their eyes: *I don't know what is going on over there, but I want some of it!*

THE KEY TO
EMBRACING FUN
· · · · · · · · · · · · · · ·
is to find ways to
UNLEASH
· · · · · · · · · · · · · · ·
your lighter side or
reconnect with your
INNER CHILD.

Fun is healthy for us. For me, fun is sharing laughter. We all define fun in our own ways, but don't forget to stop and have some real fun once in a while. It doesn't make you soft or wimpy; it makes you feel alive and happy.

To me, the lizard experience shouts, *Sam, lighten up!* If there is one thing we need more of, it is to lighten up. Can you think of one person right now who could benefit from this approach? If you can't think of anyone, then I'm betting someone else reading this might be thinking of you! Positive humor makes us feel good. It is not just standing around the water cooler telling jokes. It's embracing the lighter side of things and not magnifying those that create more stress.

I understand that there is nothing more frustrating than working or dealing with someone who is over-the-top uptight. A person like that lets his or her ego get in the way. Uptight people tend to complain and criticize more; they are not fun to be around. So what can we do? For starters, don't be like them. The key to embracing fun is to find ways to unleash your lighter side or reconnect with your inner child. The positive side effect of having some fun is creating a stronger connection between others— including customers, loved ones, and possibly even strangers at a sporting event! For example, when I go to Minnesota Vikings football games, I high-five and even hug total strangers because we are all having fun at the game!

Humor is an incredible tool for building business. One of my friends uses humor to attract new customers. He calls and leaves this voice mail to get a return call: "Hello, this is Dan. A priest, a rabbi, and a fisherman walk into a bar. If you want to hear the rest of this joke, call me back." People actually call him back to get the rest of the joke!

Have you ever walked out of the bathroom with toilet paper stuck to the bottom of your shoe, or, better yet, your pants? I have! Who knew that could be so entertaining for others? Next time you want to create a surefire laugh for your friends, family, or staff, do it on purpose. Make it ridiculous by having five feet of toilet paper dragging from your shoe or the back of your pants. Act like you don't even notice. People will roll with laughter. When someone finally tells you that toilet paper is stuck to you, just smile and say, "I know; I am saving that for later."

Collect Positive Humor and
Share It in Positive Ways

Having fun and sharing good humor with others is not about being a comedian, but rather about taking a situation and finding its lighter side to ease the stress. That's part of the lizard experience. I love to collect funny stories and share them!

Here is something I found from an anonymous author that you may like:

The Top Ten Things to Say When Caught Sleeping at Your Desk:

10. *"They told me at the blood bank this might happen."*

9. *"This is just a fifteen-minute power nap like they raved about in the time management course you sent me to."*

8. *"Whew! Guess I left the top off the Wite-Out again. You probably got here just in time."*

7. *"I wasn't sleeping! I was meditating on the mission statement and envisioning a new paradigm."*

6. *"I was testing my keyboard for drool resistance."*

5. *"I was doing a highly specific yoga exercise to relieve work-related stress. Are you discriminatory toward people who practice yoga?"*

4. *"Why did you interrupt me? I had almost figured out a solution to our biggest problem."*

3. "The coffee machine is broken..."

2. "Someone must've put decaf in the wrong pot..."

And the No. 1 best thing to say if you get caught sleeping at your desk...

1. "... in Jesus' name. Amen."

Having fun is a big priority to me. My family and I go on fishing trips, to football games, or wherever we think is fun for all of us to go. It could be as simple as watching a movie together. Some companies I have spoken for plan fun activities for employees so they can relax a bit and connect with others on a different level. As a side benefit, people enjoy where they work more, which translates into more productive, loyal employees and less turnover.

Fun is a unique way to connect with others and make a difference.

I LIVE TO LAUGH, AND I LAUGH TO LIVE.

—MILTON BERLE

THE LIZARD BECOMES YOUR LEGACY

What do you want to be remembered for? When you look back on your life, what will others remember about you? What will your legacy be? Did you use up the best of who you are, or will there be leftovers? The lizard experience was something my mom started by using her uniqueness mixed with a positive attitude. It will be something she will always be known for—hiding a toy lizard in my lasagna and setting something positive in motion that would impact many people.

We all have the ability to create a legacy for ourselves when we care enough to give the best of who we are with a positive attitude.

Your Extraspecial Signature

In the old TV show, the Lone Ranger always left behind a symbol of his greatness—a silver bullet. Zorro did something similar. Whenever he did a good deed, he left his mark, the letter Z, scratched on a wall with his sword.

I leave toy lizards that, if mixed with a positive attitude, will have a positive impact.

What do you want to be remembered for? I want to be known for my kindness and sincerity. That's part of my extraspecial signature. I like to do nice things for others. It doesn't matter if I'm at work or at home, in public or around only one other person. If the opportunity presents itself to act, I do.

This is meaningful to me because of all the people who have done kind things for me. Because of their actions, I am motivated to do the same. It's a pet peeve of mine to see rudeness. There is not a single benefit to being rude. **None.**

In fact, even when rudeness might be justified, it's better for everyone to be kind. I was once so tired during a flight home that I fell asleep on the shoulder of the woman next to me. When I woke up, I started laughing and apologized.

She might have given me a piece of her mind or even a dirty look. Instead, she smiled and said, "It was my pleasure. You are welcome to finish your nap there if you'd like."

Her gesture was sweet and sincere. It also helped that I hadn't drooled on her!

To act with kindness is to take an opportunity to build a legacy. Maybe your act of kindness is to get involved with a cause that helps children with cancer. Maybe it's being a source of encouragement for others. We've all had times when we've needed help and wondered whom we could call on.

What will your legacy be?

LEGACY STARTS WITH A HEART OF WILLINGNESS.

Building a Legacy Can Start Anywhere, Even Cleaning Toilets

The starting point to creating your legacy starts with an attitude of willingness—being willing to jump in and actively make a significant contribution. We all have special gifts we can use to make an impact, but sometimes our ego gets in the way. Being willing is doing whatever it takes. I learned this the hard way years ago during a summer camp internship.

I was jazzed to be a part of the camp's cause, which was to help young people make positive choices and grow in faith, leadership, and sportsmanship. I thought of all the ways I could use my skills and gifts to make a difference but was more than slightly shocked when I arrived and discovered that my duties included cleaning bathrooms. My enthusiasm went right out the window. My ego, pride, and fear of what to expect when cleaning those toilets got in the way. I thought it was my place to walk down to the camp director and complain. He listened and then calmly responded, "Sam, if you don't clean those toilets, who will?"

Initially, I thought of three other people who could do it.

He continued, "Everything we do here contributes to making a difference. Instead of complaining about cleaning toilets, why not do it with the right attitude? And that involves knowing you are making a difference here."

I had to think hard about what he told me. He was right: legacy starts with a heart of willingness. It's not about position, experience, rank, or skills; it's about being willing to do whatever it takes. I tried a new attitude, and it really helped. Not only did I clean those toilets, but I also made sure those bathrooms looked the best they ever had.

Don't spend your precious time asking,
"WHY ISN'T THE WORLD A BETTER PLACE?"
It will only be time wasted.
THE QUESTION TO ASK IS,
"HOW CAN I MAKE IT BETTER?"
TO THAT THERE IS AN ANSWER.
—LEO BUSCAGLIA

LET ME WRAP THINGS UP...

The lizard experience taught me some pretty simple, yet life-changing lessons. Looking back, I am thankful my mom didn't put a fake spider or snake in the lasagna! I'm not sure I could've handled that. I have, however, come to appreciate and draw upon the lessons the lizard offers.

Remember, you don't need a plastic toy to achieve more of what you desire in life. The essence of the lizard is already inside you—it just represents your uniqueness. You showed up on this planet with amazing gifts and abilities. If you apply them where you are right now with a positive attitude, you'll begin to experience more of what you want, and good things will happen!

The one trait that can keep us from moving forward or using the gifts we have is a thing called doubt. It is a killer of dreams, relationships, and opportunities. Doubt is a negative attitude that keeps us from doing our best. It makes us question our efforts and the greatness we were born with. It attacks us when we fail—through negative people or by showing up in our thoughts. *Doubt doesn't work for you... So don't employ it!*

When You Doubt Yourself, You Will Defeat Yourself

Believing in yourself works. You don't have to be perfect or compare yourself to others. Choose to be amazing just as you are!

Every day I look for opportunities to apply this lesson, to **use the best of who I am to achieve the best of what I want.** It's not about acquiring stuff. It's not about manipulating people or mimicking successful leaders. The lizard concept is about making your life—and the lives of others—worthwhile.

My hope is that you will embrace these ideas and make them your own. Give them life through your attitude and actions. It really is that simple!

WHEN YOU BELIEVE IN YOURSELF, ANYTHING IS POSSIBLE.

—SAM GLENN

ABOUT
THE AUTHOR

Sam Glenn went from working as a night janitor to becoming one of America's most renowned speakers on the subject of attitude. For the past seventeen years, Sam has been the go-to guy as the opening and closing speaker for conferences all across the country. Leaders from retail, educational, and health-care organizations such as Blue Cross Blue Shield, Walmart, AT&T, Meeting Professionals International, and the Society for Human Resource Management turn to him for counsel on creating a more engaging, positive, and enthusiastic culture for their workplaces.

Sam uses humor in his speeches to make learning new ideas fun and offers perceptive ideas that will enrich your life as a leader and as a person. Visit his website, www.SamGlenn.com, to enjoy some of his motivational videos.

To inquire about having Sam speak at your next leadership meeting or conference, email: **Sam@SamGlenn.com**